Original title:
Rosewater Rhapsodies

Copyright © 2025 Creative Arts Management OÜ
All rights reserved.

Author: Sophia Kingsley
ISBN HARDBACK: 978-1-80566-734-6
ISBN PAPERBACK: 978-1-80566-863-3

Fragrant Melodies of Solitude

In a garden where the daisies laugh,
A sneaky snail takes a bubble bath.
Petals dance with a silly sway,
While bees debate on who will play.

The sun sneezes, giving us a wink,
As butterflies gather for a quick drink.
A worm tells jokes that make us sigh,
While daisies giggle, oh so spry!

A tree swings its branches, acting coy,
Echoing whispers, oh what joy!
Raindrops join in a playful race,
While shadows make silly, funny faces.

In this whimsical world, so bright,
The moon moonwalks, what a sight!
Every flower knows how to groove,
In this joyful rhapsody, we all move.

Floral Wishes in the Twilight

Petals dance in twilight's glow,
A sneaky bee, a gentle show.
Lavender laughs as wind does tease,
While daisies play, with utmost ease.

Sunset blushes, flowers grin,
A cat's mischief leads the spin.
Tulips gossip, oh so bright,
Bringing jokes to the moonlight.

A Melody of Soft Flora

Breezes hum a tune so sweet,
Butterflies waltz with dainty feet.
Tulips tell a joke or two,
While sunflowers nod, oh so true.

Petunias giggle, tickled pink,
In gardens grand, they stop to wink.
The violets burst in joyful cheer,
As crickets croon, their tunes we hear.

Cascading Memories of Floral Bliss

Blossoms twirl in a playful swirl,
With every color, a dance unfurl.
Poppies tease the lazy bee,
While pansies wink, 'Come laugh with me!'

In the moment, laughter's bloom,
Cucumbers giggle, no hint of gloom.
Each petal a giggle, each stem a grin,
In this garden, joy's sure to win.

The Garden's Tender Whispers

Crickets chuckle, grasshoppers croon,
The daisies plot a merry tune.
Roses whisper in gentle jest,
"Why bloom alone when we're the best?"

The marigolds wear silly hats,
Spinning tales while avoiding chats.
Daffodils strut, a comical sight,
In the garden, all feels just right.

Whispers between the Blossom's Breath

In gardens where the giggles grow,
A pollen party starts to flow.
Bees bump into blooms and sway,
While flowers gossip all the day.

The daisies dance, the sun's a clown,
Tickling petals in the town.
With scents that swirl like laughter's song,
Nature hums its funny throng.

Luminous Embrace of Nature's Muse

Under a sky with winks and grins,
The sun and moon engage in spins.
They trade their hats—one bright, one blue,
And giggle as the stars accrue.

A playful breeze weaves through the trees,
Tugging leaves like pesky bees.
With every rustle, nature sighs,
In a bouquet of silly ties.

Silken Petals and Gentle Breezes

Silken petals in a breeze,
Tease the bumblebees with ease.
They buzz and flit in a dizzy dance,
Chasing scents like a clumsy romance.

The tulips laugh with colors bright,
In their floral, frolicking delight.
As butterflies don hats so grand,
They swirl like jesters in this land.

Palette of the Softly Spoken

A palette spills from nature's hand,
With colors jumbled, oh so grand.
Pinks and yellows play in rows,
Mischief hidden in their glows.

Whispers flutter like a song,
Where even thorns have laughs along.
Nature's canvas full of cheer,
Paints a picture bright and dear.

Fragrant Mornings and Moonlit Nights

Morning blooms with laughter bright,
Bees in bow ties take their flight.
Sunlight dances on petals wide,
While squirrels play hide-and-seek with pride.

Moonlight tipsy in the trees,
Whispers secrets on the breeze.
Crickets chirp a cheeky tune,
As cats perform a midnight swoon.

The Symphony of Soft Petals

A petal fell, it made a thud,
A tumbleweed of fragrant mud.
Beetles form a marching band,
While ants enlist with little hands.

The daisies giggle, how they sway,
Playing poker in the clay.
The sun brings jokes to brighten smiles,
Each bloom bursting with silly wiles.

Elixir of Dawn's Embrace

Morning coffee brewed with glee,
A splash of joy, a bumblebee.
Toast pops up, a golden knight,
Battle of flavors, oh what a sight!

The world awakens with a grin,
As roosters chime, let chaos begin.
The toast's butter, a slippery foe,
While cats are plotting their next big show.

Lullabies for a Garden Heart

In the garden, whispers play,
Lullabies from flowers sway.
A caterpillar croons a line,
While fireflies blink in dance, divine.

Napping gnomes in the shade,
Dream of pies and lemonade.
With every snore, new blooms appear,
And laughter blooms, oh what a cheer!

Flourishes of Love and Bloom

In a garden of giggles, the blossoms tease,
Little bees do the cha-cha with utmost ease.
Petals prance in the wind, wearing taffeta clothes,
While snails play the trombone, striking silly poses.

Daisies declare they're the queens of the scene,
Popping out from their beds, all shiny and clean.
Tickled by the sun's rays, they dance with delight,
Spinning stories of mischief till the fall of night.

Daydreams in Petal Hues

A dandelion whispers, "Blow me a sweet wish,"
While the violets giggle, "Make it a fish!"
Sunflowers strut, wearing shades, looking sly,
As butterflies trade secrets, floating on by.

The sky's a canvas splashed with blissful hues,
Lucid dreams play hide-and-seek in bright shoes.
Tulips crack jokes at the clumsy old pines,
While the wind takes a bow, with a flurry of signs.

The Essence of a Gentle Touch

A rose tries to wiggle, but ends up in knots,
The lilacs erupt, "Let's give it a shot!"
With petals a-flapping, they gossip away,
Creating a scene that's the talk of the day.

Laughter erupts when the buds start to sway,
A tickle of joy in a floral ballet.
With scents so enchanting, they laugh till they cry,
While the mossy old stones wink, "Oh my, oh my!"

Soiree of the Spun Silks

At a party for petals, the snips and snails dance,
With silk-draped invitations, they all take a chance.
The daisies wear bow ties, all witty and spry,
As lilies recite limericks that soar to the sky.

They toast with sweet nectar in sparkling cups,
While the cheerful old hedgehog tries filling them up.
The crickets play banjos, the frogs croon along,
At this whimsy-filled gala, all living belong.

Flowers and Dreamscapes Collide

In a world where daisies dance,
Tulips wear the latest pants.
Sunflowers laugh with mighty grace,
While violets trip in a silly race.

Dandelions puff their fluffy cheeks,
Telling jokes that last for weeks.
Petunias twirl and spin around,
In this garden, joy is found.

Lilies sing a tune off-key,
As bumblebees buzz in glee.
The petals gossip, oh so bold,
Sharing secrets never told.

A rose in shades of bright maroon,
Danced a tango with a spoon.
While the weeds chuckled from the side,
In this floral fun, there's no need to hide.

The Language of Petals Unfolds

In a bouquet where laughter thrives,
Petals chat like old-time jives.
Carnations boast their dizzy spins,
As daisies giggle, the fun begins.

A sunflower's wink, a daisy's shout,
Their silly banter leaves no doubt.
Pansies wear their party hats,
Telling jokes about the cats.

Tulips tease the sturdy ferns,
While violets plot their wild returns.
The marigolds roll on the ground,
In this petal talk, joy's abound.

Every flower has a quirk,
Even the shy ones start to smirk.
In this garden, humor grows,
With laughter blooming, anything goes.

Breath of the Garden's Heart

A breeze whispers amongst the leaves,
Tickling petals wearing sleeves.
Roses blush with playful grins,
While orchids giggle and spin wins.

Buttercups clap with sunny cheer,
As tulips stretch their arms, oh dear!
A daffodil's caper sends them rolling,
In the garden, joy is a-strolling.

Snapdragons snap, they're in a jest,
Freely mocking all the rest.
Even the ferns join the spree,
With ferny jokes, come share with me!

This leafy heart beats loud and clear,
With every chuckle, all draw near.
So dance among the buds and leaves,
Where laughter flourishes, no one grieves.

Dreams in Shades of Petal Pink

In dreams where flowers take their flight,
Petals giggle through the night.
A pink horizon starts to glow,
As blossoms play with the breeze's flow.

Cherry blossoms jump and sway,
Frolicking through the light of day.
They wear their pinks with pride so high,
Spreading smiles as they pass by.

Cosmos spin in dreamy arcs,
Turning heads with floral sparks.
Petal whispers in the air,
Each bloom's a joke with flair to spare.

Lilacs waltz, their colors bright,
Creating laughter, pure delight.
In this garden world of whimsy cold,
The petals tell tales, both funny and bold.

Whispers of the Floral Lane

In the garden, bees do buzz,
Wondering just what the fuss was.
Petals dance, a waltz so bright,
Wink at the sun, then hide from light.

A ladybug prepares for tea,
Offers biscuits, fancy and free.
The roses giggle with delight,
As frogs in suits jump left and right.

Lavish scents swirl in the air,
Who knew that flowers could be rare?
Forget-me-nots, they surely know,
One cannot bloom without a show!

So join the bloom, don't be a bore,
With floral friends, you'll want for more.
A cha-cha dance, a sunflower spin,
In this wild garden, let laughs begin!

Caresses of Lavender and Gold

Lavender fields in giggling hues,
Play hide and seek with clumsy muse.
The buttercups bow, a silly sight,
As daisies dare the clouds to fight.

In a swirl of petals, laughter flows,
Caterpillars pose in glittery clothes.
Ticklish vines climb with a grin,
While sunflowers jest, "We can't lose to spin!"

The bees wear sunglasses, oh so chic,
Trading honey secrets, laughing cheek to cheek.
Lavish days with silliness spun,
Under the banner of bright golden sun.

So let your worries drift away,
Join the flowers, let's frolic and play.
A tickle here, a giggle there,
In this meadow, joy is everywhere!

Silken Threads of Floral Passion

Dandelions toss their seeds like confetti,
While tulips plan a party quite ready.
With silken threads of sunshine spun,
The floral world is bursting with fun!

A peony in a polka dot hat,
Sways with flair, what do you think of that?
With whimsical whispers floating by,
Petals prance and giggle, oh my!

Lilies in shades of cheeky delight,
Challenge the roses to a dance-off night.
"Oh, you think you're fancy?" giggle the ferns,
As laughter rings, and the earth just turns.

Join this grand floral jubilee,
Where fun is meant for you and me.
With every bloom, a chuckle awaits,
Life's too short — just open the gates!

Memories in Every Bloom

Each flower whispers tales of old,
With secrets in petals, stories unfold.
A daisy laughs, "I knew him well,"
While violets giggle at tales they tell.

The marigolds gossip, colorful and bright,
"Mornings are better, just look at the light!"
With a swirl of petals and fragrant cheer,
A perfume of memories, always near.

When roses tease about that summer fling,
Lilies just roll their eyes, while they sing.
Every blossom a chapter, a tale so sweet,
In the garden of laughter, all friends meet.

So stroll through the blooms, have a laugh,
In this field of wonder, take the path.
Where sunshine and laughter intertwine very close,
Let's cherish these moments, for they matter most!

The Blooming Veil of Memories

In a garden of laughter, blooms bright,
The petals whisper secrets at night.
A bee in a tux, a butterfly dance,
Each fragrant encounter, a silly romance.

With daisies as hats and sunflowers cheer,
The memories frolic, year after year.
Oh, how the roses giggle and sway,
In this perfume of joy, we'll forever play.

Sweet Aroma of Forgotten Days

Nostalgia drips like syrupy dew,
Unraveling tales of mischief anew.
Petals in fedoras, tulips with flair,
The scent of old pranks fills the air.

A daisied mistake, a breezy slip,
Laughter erupts from a flower's quip.
We dance through the chaos with glee and with fun,
In a bouquet of blunders, we've only begun.

Variations in Floral Melodies

A symphony forged in colors divine,
With violets humming a wobbly line.
Tulips are crooning a jazzier tune,
As sunbeams pirouette beneath the moon.

The daisies tap dance, sprightly and spry,
While lilacs regale with a wink of the eye.
Each flower's a note in this funny parade,
Where petals compose serenades unafraid.

Secrets Linger in the Air

Amidst the blooms where secrets conspire,
The petals share tales that never tire.
A rose with a wink, a daffodil's joke,
Even thorns have a punchline to poke.

In this floral haven where giggles abound,
Every whiff is a riddle woven sound.
As whispers of blooms swirl in a cheer,
The truth is a punchline, always near.

Scented Dreams at Twilight

In twilight's glow, the flowers lean,
They giggle softly, a fragrant scene.
With petals wide, they plot and scheme,
Each petal tosses, a playful dream.

A breeze arrives, it tells a joke,
The daisies laugh, the roses choke.
A sprig of thyme whispers quite loud,
While violets dance, oh, so proud!

Laughter in the Garden

In gardens bright, the veggies talk,
With beetroot blush, they start to squawk.
Carrots giggle, roots entwined,
While cabbage snickers, oh so kind!

A sunflower winks with a sunny grin,
It starts to sway, a dance within.
Among the blooms, the laughter swells,
As every petal shares its swells.

Fragrant Echoes of Dusk

When dusk arrives, the scents collide,
With lavender laughs, they twist and glide.
The marigolds tease with playful flair,
While night-blooming joy fills the air.

A whiff of mint starts the fun,
It tickles noses, one by one.
With every breeze, a chuckle shared,
In fragrant echoes, we're all declared.

The Dance of Dewdrops

Droplets twirl on blades of grass,
With tiny giggles, they sway and pass.
A teardrop chuckles, bright and wet,
Beneath the moon, a sight to beget.

In morning's light, they leap around,
Bouncing high with every sound.
Each twinkling gem a joke to tell,
In the dance of dewdrops, all is well!

Enchanted Fragrance of Twilight

In twilight's glow, a scent awakes,
A mix of giggles and sweet mistakes.
Potions brewed in a dainty jar,
Made me think, I'm a garden star!

The bees all buzz in a silly line,
Debating if this nectar's fine.
I tried to catch one for a dance,
But all it did was take the chance.

Elixirs of Softest Petals

With petals soft as morning skies,
I brewed a blend, oh what a prize!
But when I sipped, it turned to goo,
And left me looking like a shrew!

The squirrels laughed, they had a ball,
As I stumbled, tripped, and nearly fall.
Unicorns danced in fits of glee,
As I embraced my fate, oh me!

Garden Lullabies at Dawn

At dawn the flowers softly hum,
A melody that sounds quite dumb.
With croaking frogs and chirps of birds,
It mixes up all of our words.

I tried to sing along in tune,
But ended up just sounding like a loon.
The flowers giggled, oh what a tease,
As I sang out loud to please the bees!

Nostalgia Wrapped in Blossoms

In gardens where my childhood bloomed,
I pondered all my dreams entombed.
Wrapped in petals, memories flew,
Like fragrant socks that once were new.

I sniffed a bunch, but sneezed so hard,
The thoughts took flight, they hit the yard.
The flowers chuckled, swaying with glee,
As my nose guided them, oh wee!

A Symphony of Soft Petals

In a garden where giggles grow,
Petals ripple like jokes on a flow,
Bees buzzed around in a silly dance,
While raindrops joined in with a playful chance.

Butterflies flit in a tutu so bright,
Winking at clouds in a comical flight,
Each bloom whispers secrets, oh what a sight,
As flowers chuckle under the moonlight.

The daisies are laughing, their stems all askew,
With tulips gossiping about morning dew,
"Why did the rose blush?" they tease and they twine,
"Because it saw the violets drinking sweet wine!"

Even the sun beams in laughter's embrace,
As shadows play tag, all over the place,
A symphony blooms with a witty refrain,
In a garden where joy will always remain.

Hues of Evening Blooms

Evening wraps petals in colorful swirls,
With giggles that shimmer and twirl like the girls,
Daisies in polka dots jest with the night,
While laughter erupts from the stars, oh what a sight!

The sun bids farewell with a flamboyant flair,
As night blinks awake, sending scents through the air,
Lilacs jeer at the fading, long day,
"Why so serious?" they tease in their play.

Petunias dance with a wink at the sky,
"Take off that frown, it's our time to fly!"
A riot of colors, so crazy and bold,
Without a care, just like dreaming untold.

With fuchsia and violet, the moon starts to grin,
As crickets chirp jokes, let the fun now begin,
In hues of the evening, where silliness blooms,
A symphony's song finds its way through the rooms.

Liquid Velvet on My Skin

A splash of delight on my sun-kissed arms,
Liquid velvet flows, with its magical charms,
The garden giggles, as I dare take a dip,
In silky smooth waters, oh what a trip!

Petals pouring laughter right into my drink,
Each sip a delight, making me rethink,
"Do fish wear polka dots?" I ponder, not shy,
As bees break the silence, buzzing goodbye.

With every splash, the flowers all tease,
"Who needs a bath? Just splash with a breeze!"
And slippery plants make me lose my balance,
In this whimsical dance, I find my own valiance.

With each droplet shimmering, I feel so alive,
Caught in the moment, I simply must thrive,
Liquid joy cascading from blossom to here,
A funny ballet, spreading smiles so near.

Serenade of the Silk Rose

A silk rose sways with a jig and a whirl,
Telling tall tales to the nearby pearl,
"Have you heard of the daffodil's dream?"
It's too funny to keep just a simple theme!

"Roses are red, violets cry blue,
But watch out for sunshine, it will tie up your shoe!"
With petals a-flutter and laughter so bright,
The silk rose serenades, igniting the night.

At the midnight ball, crickets play harp,
While flowers spin tunes in a garden so sharp,
Moss winks at us, with a cheeky little humor,
As shadows tap dance like a cheeky consumer.

"Why do daisies shake when they hear a good pun?"
"Because they can't handle the bloom of the fun!"
With each petal's giggle, a melody flows,
In the serenade sweet of the silk rose.

Echoes of Blossom Tendrils

Under the petals, giggles dance,
Bumbling bees with a clumsy prance.
Butterflies wear their brightest hues,
Blossoms chuckle at nature's cues.

Dewdrops wink like little eyes,
Swaying grass sings lullabies.
Wind whispers jokes to the tall trees,
Nature's humor, a breeze through leaves.

A snail in a shell takes a spin,
Wondering why the flowers grin.
The sun throws shade on a lazy cat,
While daisies laugh at a butterfly's chat.

Joy blooms where the sunlight flows,
In every petal, fun overflows.
Nature's laughter, wild and free,
A garden party for you and me.

Harvest of the Heart's Fragrance

Jars of laughter line the shelves,
Scented memories of our funny selves.
Petals swirl in a comedic waltz,
Each bloom has quirks, oh what a vault!

A laughable daisy went on a spree,
Chasing a bumblebee up a tree.
While violets try to wear a crown,
Their wilting giggles tumble down.

The carrots chuckle in the ground,
As rabbits hop with laughter abound.
Tomatoes blush at the sight of peas,
In this patch, mirth is sure to tease.

Golden sunlight brews a delight,
While strawberries joke under the light.
Each fruit a jester, in nature's court,
Harvesting laughter as a grand sport.

Midnight Serenade of Flowers

When the moonlight takes a stroll,
Flowers whisper secrets, heart and soul.
Lilies serenade with a giggly tune,
Charming the stars beneath the moon.

Crickets join in with a cheeky jest,
As petals sway and take a rest.
The night air tickles with fragrant cheer,
Dancing dreams in the atmosphere.

A tulip trips on its silken skirt,
While a nightingale gives a comical flirt.
Hydrangeas gossip, sharing the plot,
Under the gaze of a playful dot.

In the dark, laughter blooms bright,
Nature's jesters without a fright.
Celestial blooms join the fun,
As the laughter echoes 'til the sun.

Mystical Brews of Nature

In a kettle of greens, starlight brews,
Nature's chefs whip up vibrant hues.
A dash of whimsy, a sprinkle of cheer,
Every sip brings laughter near.

Fern fronds chuckle, teasing the thyme,
While basil sings in a rhythm divine.
Mint leaves giggle, so fresh and spry,
Herbs in the garden hold a sly eye.

The mushrooms dance in their earthy glen,
To the beat of raindrops, now and again.
Sage tells tales with a savory wink,
While rosemary grins with a knowing blink.

In this concoction, a potion of fun,
Nature's laughter, never done.
With each cup shared, joy multiplies,
Mystical brews under the skies.

Reveries of Floral Delight

In a garden where gnomes dance,
Flowers wear hats, given a chance.
Petals gossip, sipping dew,
Bees in tuxedos, just for the view.

Worms compose songs on a twig,
Snails race slowly, what's the big gig?
Rabbits wear shades and sip on shade,
While daisies find jokes that can't fade.

A sunflower jokes, 'I'm tall, it's true!'
But can't see the tiny ants in a queue.
They march in a line with such pride,
Saying, 'We're the best, just can't hide!'

So let's dance with blooms all around,
With laughter and joy that abound.
Nature's a stage with a quirky twist,
In the garden, a surrealist's list.

The Allure of Nature's Kiss

Breezes whisper secrets sweet,
Butterflies wear their finest feet.
Roses chuckle, tickled by air,
Tulips giggle, with pink flair.

A squirrel tells tales of a nut,
As daisies roll, but stay in a rut.
Crickets play tunes for a footpath waltz,
While the sunbeams make silly jolts.

A potted plant's crown slips askew,
Pretending it's fancy in morning dew.
Bees buzzing loudly, claim 'We're the crew!'
Saying, 'With pollen, there's much we can do!'

Beneath the trees, laughter rings clear,
Every petal's got a joke to steer.
Nature's a prankster, don't you see?
In this garden, we all shout with glee!

Petals Touched by the Sun

Beneath bright skies, petals come alive,
Bumblebees dance, trying to jive.
Tulips wink, 'We're fashionably late!'
While violets make plans to create.

The daisies plan a wild parade,
While roses and pansies play charade.
A squirrel dons a crown made of leaves,
And jests about picking up thieves!

Sunflowers stretch, with necks so long,
Hoping to join the wind's merry song.
'I'm the tallest!' one proudly claims,
While others laugh, calling cute names.

So join this cheer, as nature sings,
With every petal, this joy it brings.
In fields of whimsy, nothing but fun,
Where laughter blooms brightly, kissed by the sun.

Cascades of Enchanted Fragrance

In a blossom kingdom, fairies abide,
Each one with a scent they can't hide.
Jasmine sings, 'Take a whiff, do you see?'
While lilacs giggle, 'Just let it be!'

Petals flutter like feathers in flight,
Trailing scents that smell oh-so-right.
Honeysuckle with a wink and a nod,
Says, 'Trust me, this perfume is a prod!'

Noses twitch, as mint leaves tease,
Lavender laughs, 'Let's all just breeze!'
As daisies declare with mischievous charm,
'Who needs a hug when we can disarm?!'

So dance through the scents, let joy collide,
In the garden where fragrances glide.
Embrace the quirky, the sweet, and the fun,
In this floral fairy tale, everyone's won!

Petals of Promise

In the garden where giggles play,
A flower sneezed, and what a day!
Petals danced in wild delight,
As bees buzzed in a dippy flight.

A snail wore shades, thought it quite cool,
He slid on leaves like a slippery fool.
The sun winked down with a mocking grin,
While flowers whispered of mischief within.

A daisy told jokes, a tulip laughed loud,
The humor hidden beneath the crowd.
Who knew petals could have such fun?
In their world, of laughter, they're never done.

So, skip through the blooms, feel the cheer,
In a silly garden, nothing's unclear!
With every breeze, let the laughter swell,
In this petal parade, all's well, all's well!

Whispered Dreams in Bloom

In a sunlit patch, dreams softly sigh,
A bumblebee grumbled, oh my, oh my!
He tripped on a stem, did a slapstick fall,
And petals erupted in giggles for all.

The tulips were gossiping, shades of red,
Spilling secrets that all flowers dread.
A daffodil chortled, "What a grand spree!"
As wind tickled thoughts, wild and free.

A rogue dandelion danced with a breeze,
Then sneezed out its seeds, oh, what a tease!
They floated like wishes across the blue,
Telling stories of dreams that could come true.

So if you find blooms with a twinkle in hue,
Laugh with the petals, join in the crew!
In this fragrant revelry, joy is the tune,
Where dreams in bloom hum an old silly tune.

Scented Serenade at Dusk

As evening fell with a whispering breeze,
Petals began their frolicking tease.
A rose wore a hat that was oh so round,
While marigolds jived, spinning 'round and 'round.

The night sky chuckled as stars took their place,
As daisies danced in a silly race.
With laughter aplenty, they sang out loud,
Creating a symphony that wrapped the crowd.

A ladybug played the tambourine grand,
While violets clapped, oh so unplanned!
Lavender hummed a tune sweetly bright,
In this scented music, all wrongs felt right.

So let us sway in this fragrant delight,
As petals perform in the soft moonlight.
Join their serenade, silly and bold,
In a tapestry where laughter unfolds!

Dew-Kissed Echoes

Morning dew glistened on petals awake,
As buttercups giggled, "Let's have a break!"
They played hide and seek with the buzzing bees,
While petals dropped jokes on the soft morning breeze.

A cheeky sunflower asked, "What's the buzz?"
"Just blooming ideas!"—then shared with a fuzz.
Their laughter echoed through shrubberies wide,
As the garden erupted in joyful pride.

A bouncy bumblebee did a hiccuping spin,
As geraniums chuckled, "Let's do it again!"
In this dewy kingdom where fun lives high,
Every flower poses with a wink of an eye.

So wander in wonder through this floral song,
Where dew-kissed echoes play all day long.
Join the merriment, forget all your woes,
In a whimsical world where laughter just grows!

The Aura of Distant Blooms

In a garden full of cheer,
Butterflies dance without fear.
Petals giggle in the breeze,
Whisper secrets to the trees.

Bees buzz with a playful sigh,
Chasing dreams that float on high.
Laughter echoes from the sprout,
While worms wiggle, roundabout.

Sunlight sprinkles on the ground,
Where silly gnomes are often found.
They trip and tumble, oh so spry,
Always wearing a bowtie.

Tulips strike a funny pose,
Tickling toes of all the rose.
In this world of blooms and fun,
Every moment's like a pun.

Poems of the Blossoming Air

In the air, a sweet delight,
Breezes giggle, what a sight.
Flowers hum in joyful play,
Swaying gently through the day.

Clouds peek down with sly grins,
As squirrels chase their fuzzy wins.
A bumblebee in silly flight,
Tricks a daffodil in bright.

Caterpillars wear their hats,
Wiggling 'round in acrobat.
Daisies wink with sunny flair,
As frogs croak songs into the air.

Petunias wear a polka dot,
Twirling skirts, they dance a lot.
In this garden, laughter blooms,
Chasing away all the glooms.

A Tapestry Woven of Scents

A tapestry of scents unfolds,
Laughter from the petals holds.
Lavender tickles the shy breeze,
While daisies laugh and hug the trees.

Basil joking with the thyme,
In their quirky, greeny rhyme.
Cinnamon twirls with giddy cheer,
While rose hips roll and disappear.

Honey drips from playful bears,
Who are never short on dares.
Each blossom shares a silly tale,
With a giggle, never stale.

Nectar flows in joyful streams,
As nature weaves its silly dreams.
In this fragrant, funny space,
Every bloom wears a smiling face.

Moments Captured in a Garden

Moments captured, oh so bright,
In a garden filled with light.
Worms are wriggling in a race,
Squirrels wearing silly grace.

Petals blush and wink at bees,
While birds joke in swaying trees.
Every corner brings a grin,
As flowers dance and spin within.

Snapdragons snap with clever flair,
Tickling blooms without a care.
Grinning daisies in the sun,
Every day's a laugh-filled run.

Buttercups in sunny row,
Chasing giggles to and fro.
In this patch of leafy glee,
Every moment's pure jubilee.

Chasing the Blooming Dawn

In gardens where the laughter grows,
The sun peeks through like a clown's big nose.
Honeybees juggle, buzzing with flair,
While flowers giggle, dancing in the air.

Chasing dew drops as they roll and sway,
The morning light can't steal our play.
We race the shadows, whispering cheer,
As petals throw confetti, spreading good cheer.

Harmony in the Petal's Caress

A moth flutters by, wearing a bright tie,
While daisies gossip, oh my, oh my!
Twirling in circles, the blooms shake their heads,
Planting good jokes in their leafy beds.

The tulips burst out, in colorful dress,
Holding a soirée, they dress to impress.
With pollen and laughter, they create a scene,
Their petals a stage, for the jester's routine.

Veils of Mist and Fragrance

In a shroud of mist, the daisies plot,
Sneaking up gently, playing on the spot.
Whispers of sprinkles, a prankster's delight,
As they tickle the noses of passersby, what a sight!

The lilacs concoct a sweet perfume,
That draws in the bees, it's quite the costume.
With flutters and giggles, the petals parade,
While the grass holds its belly, laughing, dismayed.

The Caress of Gossamer Dreams

A bumblebee winks, with glistening eyes,
As butterflies swirl, like colorful pies.
Tickled by breezes, the blossoms all sway,
While sunbeams applaud, joining the play.

Dreams weave through petals, weaving and twirling,
Each flower a dancer, oh, how they're swirling!
With giggles of sunshine, and quips from the dew,
The garden's a stage, and we join in too!

Songs of the Floral Minstrels

Petals dance to a tune so sweet,
Buzzing bees tap their tiny feet.
A butterfly flits, but what a sight,
It tripped on a stem and soared in fright!

Daisies jiggle in a breezy spin,
While tulips giggle, a rosy grin.
Laughter blossoms in the vibrant air,
As the sun peers in with a teasing stare.

Lilies lean in and tell a joke,
But the roses blush, their humor broke.
A daffodil snorts, a playful shout,
"Maybe we're flowers, but we're fun, no doubt!"

So sing with glee, let worries flee,
In this garden stage, we'll be carefree!
A symphony of color, a whimsical mess,
The floral minstrels, forever a jest!

Caress of the Evening Dew

Twilight drapes with a shimmering veil,
The night's soft breath tells a funny tale.
Dewdrops giggle as they cling to blades,
"Don't slip too much, or we'll throw parades!"

Moonbeams wink at the sleepy blooms,
Chuckles rise from the nighttime glooms.
A snail sprints past, it's slow but sly,
"I'm training hard for a race to the sky!"

Crickets chirp rhymes, they croon and sigh,
As fireflies dance, oh my, oh my!
In whispered tones, the petals confide,
"We're better in numbers, come take a ride!"

So let the night bring its silly charms,
With laughter wrapped in the softest arms.
Under the stars, we'll sway and gleam,
In the caress of dew, we live the dream!

Soliloquy of Scented Silhouettes

In the shadowy dance of the pictured floor,
The scents compose, and the petals roar.
A jasmine giggles, a hint of sass,
"Keep your petals safe, don't let them pass!"

Lavender leans in, whispers a tune,
"Do you smell that? It's just perfume!"
While violets blush, and lilacs beam,
They gather close for a fragrant dream.

But wait! A gust ruffles the scene,
"Who sneezed?" says the garden, in unison, keen.
A dainty fern, with a flick of its frond,
"Just spreading cheer, in this scented pond!"

So let us sway in silhouettes' art,
With fragrant giggles, we shall not part.
Label us silly, but we reign supreme,
In this olfactory world, we're living the dream!

Harmonies of the Twilight Garden

In the twilight garden, a chorus begins,
With petals opening, the fun never thins.
A sunflower croons with a voice quite bold,
"Watch me outshine, this story unfolds!"

A peony pouts, with a dramatic flair,
"Why bloom all alone when we've friendship to share?"
The daisies join in with a hop and a skip,
They twirl and then trip on the same leafy tip!

The wind joins the song, a breezy delight,
"Let's dance to the rhythm of stars in the night!"
The garden buzzes, with laughter in tones,
As fireflies flash like glittery phones.

So sway to the tunes, let's revel and sway,
In twilight's embrace, we'll laugh and we'll play.
A melody crafted from color and cheer,
In the harmonies sweet, we've nothing to fear!

Crystalline Petals in the Moonlight

In the garden, petals glow,
Making shadows dance and flow.
A bee in tux, buzzing with flair,
Sipping nectar without a care.

The daisies giggle, swirling bright,
Claiming they can outshine the night.
A snail's slow crawl is quite the sight,
Wagers on who'll win this flight.

But the moon just hangs, serene,
Watching all this silly scene.
With whispered laughs, it keeps track,
Of floral pranks, there's no lack!

As dawn approaches, petals yawn,
Dreaming softly until the morn.
For every night brings tales anew,
In this garden, fun as dew.

The Odyssey of Blossoms Wandered

Once a bud set out to roam,
Seeking laughter far from home.
Poppies chuckled, 'Don't be shy!'
'We'll show you how to drift and fly!'

Through meadows lush, they danced in glee,
Waving at the bumblebee.
'Is that a flower or a tree?'
Asked a butterfly, 'Oh, can it be?'

With twirling vines, they spun about,
Teaching clouds what friendship's about.
The sun chuckled, a playful tease,
'Last one to bloom must bend the knees!'

Finally, tired, they found a place,
With daisies laughing in embrace.
Their journey told in petal flight,
A tale of joy, both day and night.

Harmonizing with Nature's Breath

In the forest, leaves sway bright,
Chorusing songs deep in the night.
A frog with dreams of pop star fame,
Croaks a tune, despite the shame.

Grassy blades tap dance in tune,
Complaining squirrels sing to the moon.
Sunflowers nod, keeping the beat,
While crickets step with tiny feet.

The rhythm pulls the stars so close,
Each twinkle adds to nature's prose.
A giggle floats from tree to tree,
As squirrels juggle acorns with glee.

But one brave leaf, caught in a spin,
Yells, 'Hold on tight, here we begin!'
A whirlwind laugh, around they twirl,
Nature's breath in a comic swirl.

Silk and Scent Beneath the Stars

Under the stars, so soft and grand,
Petals dream in a fragrant band.
With scented whispers, they unite,
Creating riddles, oh, what a sight!

A ladybug spins tales so tall,
Saying, 'I'm the fairest of them all!'
But the roses cheer, 'Have you seen?
Our perfume's more divine, no glean!'

The jasmine winks, a sly little tease,
'How many blooms does it take to please?'
While violets giggle, tip-toe around,
In this world where joy is found.

As night draws near, a chorus starts,
Nature's humor fills our hearts.
In petals' dance and scent's embrace,
Life's a joke in this floral space.

Twilight Dances among Thorns

In twilight's grip, the petals sway,
A dancing bear in the garden's bay.
Thorns laugh out loud, waving their spines,
While the bees argue over sweet, silly lines.

Mice in polka dots throw a grand ball,
Spinning around like they're having a brawl.
Crickets chirp jokes under the moon's glow,
While the daisies giggle at the show below.

A cat in a tux funds a thistle's cause,
Handing out punch to the crowd with a pause.
"Who invited the hedgehogs?" someone will crow,
As the waltz of the weeds steals the evening's flow.

So dance here tonight, with laughter and jest,
In this wild, thorny place where we all feel blessed.
Embrace the odd, let your spirits lift high,
For twilight brings mischief right from the sky.

Nectar of the Fading Sun

The sun dips low, a sticky sweet treat,
While bugs in tuxedos shuffle their feet.
Lemonade rain falls in a citrusy splash,
As ants do the limbo in a full-on flash.

Flavors collide like a carnival fight,
Hummingbirds gossip, sipping with delight.
Petunias shake hands with the clover patch,
Whispering secrets, oh time to detach!

Buzzing around, the moths throw confetti,
While butterflies croon, "This nectar is petty!"
But a wise old toad says with a grin,
"Belly laughs matter more than the win!"

As shadows dance long, the day disappears,
With nectar so rich, let's toast with good cheers!
Riding the waves of a last light's embrace,
Fun drips from petals, a wild, silly race.

Echoes from the Floral Abyss

From the depths of blooms, a chuckle rolls out,
Roses play poker while the daisies shout.
A sunflower reclines, sporting shades of pure gold,
And whispers to violets, "I'm too cool to be bold."

Marigolds giggle, teasing the bees,
"Catch us a winner in a fit of unease!"
While tulips plot strategies, all in good fun,
To outsmart the petals and claim the sun.

A daffodil sings with an off-key tone,
As the crowd of blooms cheers in a floral zone.
"Let's hold a parade on this mischievous day,
For laughter in petals keeps sorrow at bay!"

Echoes and laughter abound from within,
In this whimsical world, let the oddness begin!
With every sweet giggle that blossoms at dark,
Echoes of joy leave behind a bright mark.

Veils of Silk and Surrender

Silk threads weave tales in the soft evening mist,
Crickets hold vows on a garden's twist.
A moth in a tutu starts dancing with grace,
While the roses blush in their silken embrace.

A jester bee buzzes, quite full of himself,
Balanced on petals like a jolly old elf.
"Fear not," he declares with a playful spin,
"Embrace all your quirks, let the laughter begin!"

Daisies don wigs, playing dress-up tonight,
As a gaggle of insects finds joy in the light.
Twists of the wind whisper secrets anew,
In this garden of folly, where dreams come true.

So lift up your hearts, let your spirits take flight,
In silk veils of laughter that shimmer so bright.
For surrender to joy is the grandest of arts,
In the dance of the flowers, oh, where it all starts!

Ephemeral Beauty in Stillness

In a garden of dreams, I found a sprout,
It practiced its dance, all wobbly and proud.
With petals that giggled, and roots that would trip,
It told me of love, with a comical quip.

The tulips got jealous, they strutted in clumps,
Bouncing like ballerinas, all twirls and all bumps.
But daisies just laughed, in their innocent way,
Saying, "We're all beautiful, come join the play!"

Butterflies swooped in with a wink and a tease,
Each flutter a whisper that carried the breeze.
The sun threw a party, with shadows as guests,
And laughter erupted, in nature's great fest.

So let's sip the nectar, and giggle a while,
Amidst blooms of pure folly, let's linger and smile.
For in this sweet folly, we find that we're free,
Waltzing with flowers, come dance here with me!

Bouquet of Forgotten Wishes

In a vase on the shelf, sat wishes galore,
Once vivid and grand, now they snore and ignore.
The hydrangeas whispered, with petals so shy,
While cosmos just chuckled, 'We'll never say bye!'

A daisy, forlorn, pondered what might have been,
"I wished for a ride on a magpie's old wing."
But violets winked back, 'Don't pout in the shade!
We'll concoct a new dream, let's parade in the glade!'

The lilies then chimed in, with a giggle so bright,
"Let's throw a grand party, and dance through the night!"
From sunlight to shadows, the wishes awoke,
With laughter and joy, like a whimsical joke.

So gather your thoughts in this wacky bouquet,
Though some dreams may drift, don't let them decay.
We'll plant seeds of laughter, let them grow wild,
In gardens of whimsy, forever beguiled!

Petals in the Breeze

Petals floated by, with a tickle and tease,
They dashed against faces, riding soft summer breeze.
The rose laughed aloud, as it lost a pink leaf,
"Aiming for laughter is my favorite belief!"

A daffodil blurted, "Why don't we do flips?"
While a nearby peony practiced some tips.
The sun peeked through giggles, tickling each bud,
Creating a whirlpool of whimsical fun flood.

With bees as the band, humming tunes oh so sweet,
Every garden could hear the delightful heartbeat.
The violets joined in with their catchy refrain,
Dancing petals and petals, a merry champagne!

In the chaos of cheer, nothing's quite out of sync,
Even weeds joined the chorus, all smiling, don't think!
A cheeky old fern shared its secrets with glee,
In fields of pure nonsense, come dance, wild and free!

Whispered Secrets of the Bloom

Under stars' silly gaze, blooms concoct schemes,
Whispers of nonsense float on night's dreamy beams.
A carnation winked sly, said, "What's black and white?"
"An unhappy zebra?!" it laughed with delight.

Chrysanthemums giggled, their petals like bells,
Reciting the tales of the flowers' great spells.
Forget-me-nots sighed, "Good luck, staying small,"
While orchids declared, "We're the fairest of all!"

A lily dove into the brightest of dreams,
"Let's float on our petals, bring back summer beams!"
With laughter that sparkled like dew in the night,
They conjured up laughter, a whimsical sight.

So listen intently, for blooms have a tale,
Of petals and giggles, of love without fail.
In the garden of secrets, where joy finds its room,
Come wander, come frolic, amidst the sweet bloom!

Tantalizing Whispers in the Air

A breeze snuck in, oh what a tease,
It tickles my nose, it dances with ease.
A scent so sweet, it makes me grin,
I swear it whispers, 'Come join in!'

But wait, what's that? A bee's in flight,
He buzzes around, he's quite the sight.
With petals in his tiny paws,
He's got my heart, despite the claws!

The petals fall like candy rain,
I dodge and weave, I'm hard to train.
A giggle here, a chortle there,
Nature's joke, a lovely scare!

So here I sit, a fool with glee,
With fragrant pranks swirling around me.
In floral chaos, I take my stand,
A merry fool in a blooming land.

Petal-Laden Memories

Once I tripped on a garden path,
Laughter spilled like a bubbly bath.
A slippered foot upon a bloom,
Who knew flowers could seal my doom?

I hear the flowers gossip low,
'Look at him, down he goes!' they crow.
With petals stuck all in my hair,
I made a throne, but don't you dare!

Gather 'round, let's share a laugh,
As I present my floral staff.
With laughter ringing, pure delight,
I'm king today in a flowery fight!

So here's to blooms that bring us cheer,
And silly slips that we hold dear.
With memories sweet like honeyed wine,
In petals wrapped, we will all shine.

Veins of Color in the Clouds

Look at the sky, a painter's dream,
With colors swirling in a cream.
They mix and mingle, laughing free,
I'm sure they're chatting, just like me!

Oh, to be a cloud, what a life!
To drift and float without any strife.
But then I think, oh dear, oh no,
What if I rain? What a show!

Imagine the splash, a puddle bright,
Where kids will dance with pure delight.
Each drop a giggle, each splash a cheer,
Nature's prankster, bringing us near!

So let's lift our heads, as colors bloom,
With laughter's echo, forget the gloom.
In veins of joy painted in the sky,
We'll chase the colors and learn to fly.

The Alchemy of Floral Sighs

In a garden filled with silly vibes,
I swear I heard a flower jive.
Twisting roots in a playful dance,
They beckon the sun for a chance!

The daisies giggled, the roses rolled,
Their secret tales having been told.
With petals waving like little flags,
They're charming pranksters, joyous brags!

Oh, to mix up a potion sweet,
A blend of laughter, a fragrant treat.
With echoes of joy swirling around,
It's alchemy found in nature's sound!

So grab a bloom and wear a grin,
Join the magic, let the fun begin.
In the breezy garden full of sighs,
Find the laughter where the flower lies!

The Harmony of Hidden Gardens

In gardens where the gnomes conspire,
With laughter blooming like a choir,
Petunias whisper silly jokes,
While daisies giggle at the folks.

A squirrel juggles acorns with flair,
A flower thinks they're a millionaire,
They dance beneath a sunlit sky,
While butterflies just flutter by.

The tulips tease the dandelions,
And roses wear their finest lion,
The bees buzz loud, a raucous tune,
While poppies laugh and chase the moon.

In this lush realm, all woes depart,
Each bloom's a secret, each leaf an art,
In harmony, they prance and sway,
A funny garden, come what may.

Dreams Woven in Fragrance

In sleepy meadows, dreams take flight,
With scents that twirl like stars at night,
A lilac whispers rhymes so neat,
While violets tap their tiny feet.

The lavender schemes with a cheeky grin,
While poppies snicker, oh where to begin?
Dreams drift like pollen on a breeze,
Chasing each other with laughter and ease.

A daffodil claims it's the best at jokes,
While the roses say, 'We're the fancy folks!'
In this olfactory comedy delight,
Each petal plays, from morning till night.

They plot to tease the passing bees,
With fragrant tales that swirl and tease,
Beneath the sun, a fragrant spree,
In dreams united, wild and free.

A Tapestry of Blossoms

A tapestry spun of colors bright,
With laughter woven into the night,
The marigolds tell wild tales,
While zinnias dance in puffy veils.

An orchid yawns, says, 'What a day!'
While petunias chant, 'Let's frolic and play!'
Each bloom is vibrant, full of cheer,
Creating joy, spreading it near.

In this patchwork garden, fun's the aim,
The flowers chase each other in a game,
The lavender spins, a dizzy delight,
While daisies crack jokes with all their might.

Laughter blooms in sunlit seams,
A canvas painted with fragrant dreams,
In every corner, mirth and jest,
This tapestry yields the very best!

Serenade of the Scented Breeze

A serenade sung by flowers' glee,
With breezes tickling the tallest tree,
The elderflower hums a cheery tune,
As honeysuckle moons like a cartoon.

The petal brigade parades with pride,
While marrows giggle, can't help but hide,
Under the shade, they form a band,
With hedgehogs playing drums so grand.

The lilacs laugh till the sun goes down,
While daisies craft a perfume crown,
In this fragrant orchestra composed,
Even the thorns are humorously posed.

Together they weave a whimsical song,
In the scented breeze, where all belong,
Mirth spills over in petals and leaves,
A garden chorus that never grieves.

Mirth in the Petal's Caress

In gardens where the daisies play,
A squirrel juggles nuts all day.
The sunbeams dance on every leaf,
While giggles bloom beyond belief.

Butterflies wear stripes that clash,
A laugh erupts with every splash.
The bees, they hum a silly tune,
As flowers sway beneath the moon.

The roses wink and tease the bee,
"Come take a sip, you're welcome, see?"
Dandelions drift in the breeze,
Whispering secrets with such ease.

The petals giggle, soft and bright,
They throw a party every night.
In nature's jest, we laugh and twirl,
In petals' grip, we find our world.

Palettes of Soft Serenity

A palette splashed with grainy cheer,
Where daisies laugh and pop like beer.
The tulips pout, their colors boast,
While lilacs giggle, pleased the most.

In gardens wide, the sun did cheer,
As butterflies twirled with no fear.
Potatoes dream of being fries,
While carrots peek with curious eyes.

The violets crack a joke or two,
And poppies wink, say, "How do you?"
Five bumblebees in funny hats,
Buzz through blooms, where laughter spats.

The wind, it swirls like playful sprites,
Dancing through the leaf's delights.
With every gust, a chuckle flies,
In nature's arms, the joy complies.

Fables Written in Blooming Colors

The daisies tell tales of a knight,
Who fought the weeds with all his might.
The tulips sing, they know the score,
While garden gnomes roll on the floor.

Each bloom's a bard with tales to weave,
Of daring stunts you'd not believe.
The daisies wink with petals wide,
As sunflowers sway in silly pride.

The roses prance in polka spots,
And daffodils tie funny knots.
They gather round, both gnome and bloom,
To share their tales amid the gloom.

Under the moon, the laughter spills,
As fireflies dance with joyful thrills.
In colors bright, the stories hum,
In vibrant hues, a jubilee's drum.

The Sunkissed Shadow of Flora

In shadows deep, where flowers sneak,
A cat in boots begins to speak.
He tells of frogs who wear bow ties,
And turtles as the wise old spies.

The daisies spin like tops in glee,
While roses rhyme in melody.
The shadows sway beneath the trees,
As laughter wafts upon the breeze.

The sun dips low, the laughter glows,
With petal hats and dance that flows.
Each bloom a clown in hidden jest,
Where nature gathers for a fest.

In flora's realm, the jokes collide,
As critters join the joyful ride.
With every hue and every sound,
A silly world of fun is found.

www.ingramcontent.com/pod-product-compliance
Lightning Source LLC
Chambersburg PA
CBHW072145200426
43209CB00051B/499